Incredible
Fireflies

By Susan Ashley

Gareth Stevens
Publishing

Please visit our website, www.garethstevens.com. For a free color catalog of all our high-quality books, call toll free 1-800-542-2595 or fax 1-877-542-2596.

Library of Congress Cataloging-in-Publication Data

Ashley, Susan.
Incredible fireflies / Susan Ashley.
    p. cm. — (The incredible world of insects)
Includes index.
ISBN 978-1-4339-4584-7 (pbk.)
ISBN 978-1-4339-4585-4 (6-pack)
ISBN 978-1-4339-4583-0 (library binding)
1. Fireflies—Juvenile literature. I. Title.
QL596.L28A843 2012
595.76′44—dc22

                                    2010035222

New edition published 2012 by
Gareth Stevens Publishing
111 East 14th Street, Suite 349
New York, NY 10003

New text and images this edition copyright © 2012 Gareth Stevens Publishing

Original edition published 2004 by Weekly Reader® Books
An imprint of Gareth Stevens Publishing
Original edition text and images copyright © 2004 Gareth Stevens Publishing

Designer: Daniel Hosek
Editors: Mary Ann Hoffman and Kristen Rajczak

Photo credits: Cover, p. 1 James Jordan Photography/Flickr/Getty Images; pp. 5, 11 © Robert & Linda Mitchell; p. 7 Brand X Pictures/Getty Images; p. 9 Paulo De Oliveira/Photolibrary/Getty Images; p. 13 © Bill Beatty/Visuals Unlimited; p. 15 Steven Puetzer/Photographer's Choice/Getty Images; p. 17 Michael Durham/Getty Images; p. 19 © J. E. Lloyd, University of Florida; p. 21 Shutterstock.com.

Printed in the United States of America

CPSIA compliance information: Batch #CS11GS: For further information contact Gareth Stevens, New York, New York at 1-800-542-2595.

Contents

Boldface words appear in the glossary.

Lighting Up the Night

On summer nights, tiny lights flash on and off in the air. The lights zig and zag. These are the bodies of male fireflies. They glow in the dark as they fly through the air.

4

Not Flies

Fireflies are beetles, not flies. They are insects with two pairs of wings. They have two hard front wings and two thin back wings.

The hard front wings guard the firefly's body and its two back wings. The firefly uses its back wings to fly.

front
wings

back
wings

9

Body Parts

The firefly has three main body parts. They are the head, **thorax**, and **abdomen**. The abdomen holds the **chemicals** that make the glow we see.

thorax

head

abdomen

11

Busy at Night

Fireflies are busy at night. They fly after sunset. They rest during the day.

Oh, That Glow!

Fireflies glow to get the attention of **mates**. Males flash light while they fly. Females on the ground flash back.

15

Glowworms

After the males and females mate, female fireflies lay eggs in the ground. The eggs **hatch**. **Larvae** crawl out. They eat a lot and glow. They are called glowworms!

Becoming a Firefly

A larva stops eating. It covers its body with a hard white shell. It becomes a **pupa**.

Inside the shell, the pupa grows wings. It comes out of the shell as a firefly.

Glossary

abdomen: the back part of an insect's body

chemical: matter that causes a change in something

hatch: to come out of an egg

larva: the stage between egg and pupa. The plural is "larvae."

mate: one of two animals that come together to make babies

pupa: the stage between larva and adult

thorax: the middle part of an insect's body

For More Information

Books

Helget, Nicole Lea. *Fireflies*. Mankato, MN: Creative Education, 2008.

Hudak, Heather C. *Fireflies*. New York, NY: Weigl Publishers, 2009.

Web Sites

Fireflies
cougar.collegiate-va.org/lower/first/fireflies.htm
Read facts about fireflies and see a close-up picture of a firefly.

Fireflies
www.whiteriverwatchers.org/FireFlies.htm
Learn where fireflies live, what they eat, and why they glow. View photos of fireflies.

Index